Spiritual Poems
of Encouragement for
the Soul

Michelle Stadard

Pure Thoughts Publishing, LLC

Spiritual Poems of Encouragement for Your Soul

Spiritual Poems of Encouragement for Your Soul

The information provided herein is stated to be truthful and consistent, in that any liability, in terms of inattention or otherwise, by any usage or abuse of any policies, processes, or directions contained within is the solitary and utter responsibility of the recipient reader. Under no circumstances will any legal responsibility or blame be held against the publisher for any reparation, damages, or monetary loss due to the information herein, either directly or indirectly.

Respective authors own all copyrights not held by the publisher.

The information herein is offered for informational purposes solely, and is universal as so. The presentation of the information is without contract or any type of guarantee assurance.

Spiritual Poems of Encouragement for Your Soul

ISBN: 978-1-943409-14-3

Spiritual Poems of Encouragement for Your Soul

Table of Contents

ACKNOWLEDGEMENTS

I would like to take the time to thank God for inspiring me and unlocking the gift of poetry. To: My husband Odimir Stadard and three wonderfully amazing children Othello, Omani, and Omar thank you for pushing and standing by my side in pursing my dreams. I would like to thank my mother Diane Williams and my father Rockie Williams Sr. for always believing in me, and encouraging me to always push toward the stars. To my sister Donna Williams's thank you for always being the support system when I need you.

Chapter 1: Reality without Jesus

I wrote this particular poem in that I needed to rededicate my life back to God. I was living a double life; I was trying to live a life of sin and a life of righteousness. I wanted to dance for Satan all during the week and some on the weekends, and be totally committed to God on Sundays. God will not have it both ways, either you are going to do right and serve him completely or do wrong and serve Satan. The word of God tells us in his word "'I know your works: you are neither cold nor hot. Would that you were either cold or hot! So, because you are lukewarm, and neither hot nor cold, I will spit you out of my mouth. (Rev 3:15-16) I was in need of a serious wakeup call and reality Check through Jesus.

Reality

Jesus said I'm the way the truth and the light, and many still choose to ignore and ignite the flame of hate that will destroy the chances of that eternal fate and issue an everlasting expiration date because when you are dead it's just too late. You are forgotten only a memory people crying RIP and some lady sadly singing "My God nearer to thee… You are no longer pondering the chances you had to get it right and seal the deal. You are headed for hell and it's all surreal.

The countless voices echoing in the darkness of no end, Wait! Can somebody please stop this horrific tormenting? As I awake from this terrible dream I find myself trembling on my knees. My heart began to skip another beat as I repent I thank God for awakening me only to face what could have been my new reality without Jesus.

Reality Check

Chapter 2: The Lord on my side

The next poem I "ENTITLED IT "If it had not been for the lord ON MY SIDE. I began to reflect on the things God brought me out of. I've almost lost all of my right toes being disobedient, I have been in two car accidents, I have almost been shot close range in the military. I was hospitalized due to little and almost no platelets in my body. The devil had his traps in place and was literally trying to take me out before I could answer the call. I began to see how each time he made a way for me by catering to my every need in sparing my life and not allowing all of the terrible things to utterly destroy my life. I thank him for being on my side, for if he had not been there for me, I truly can say I don't know where I would be. Psalms 124

The Lord on my side

If it had not been for the lord who was on my
side I'd probably died a long time ago.
Remembering just a youngling riding on a
bicycle foot got caught in the chain of a bicycle
almost lost half of my toes, sitting in the hospital.
My mama crying wishing I'd listen to her when
she told me no. I think back in 1999 still in my
prime Riding down the tram rd. last words I'm
remembering was lord have mercy on my soul. I
didn't even realize lost totally control which
shifted the car into overload.

The car landed face up onto the slippery road, I didn't notice the angel on the opposite side of the road came and attended to me. I truly thank God who was truly on my side for once again remembering me. Now I'm a soldier in Uncle Sam's army on the rifle range with my m16 waiting to get shook down. One of the soldiers' stood directly behind me last command given was turn your weapons simultaneously on blast. The bullet missed my head by a few inches oh and in 2008 did I forget to mention I began to lose my platelets I began to pray and God healed me. I thank the lord for being on my side shielding and protecting me.

Chapter 3: JORDAN'S BLUE

The next poem for me was touching; I dedicated it to one of my Friend's Jamil Jordan. I had the privilege to have served with her in the military. In memory of her son Baby J. Jordan and I became very close, and was about to embark another journey in life, our first pregnancies. We conceived both of our children in February 2003 I had my son February 24th and she had hers on the 26th, we were so happy. We began to make it an everyday day children's date thing. In allowing our children bonding the two of us became close. One day Jordan did not show up and I became worried, I called and no one answered, I later found out that Jordan's son had passed away. My heart melted I did not know what to do but, just pray for my friend that God would see her through.

JORDAN'S BLUE

Jordan's blue I wish I knew then I could have comforted you or even talked to you I was just sitting home wondering what I could do, trying to figure out why Jordan was blue? Born two days apart when I got the call the news almost stopped my heart. I didn't know where to start. The day you never showed up I knew something was wrong; our babies' young still had a bond that was strong. I prayed God strengthen you. Baby J it was not easy loosing you everybody from Knox still be missing you. God loved you the most and had better plans for you. I wish you knew how much your mom loved and cared for you. I know God will comfort her, to see her through and change
This mood.

Chapter 4: Lord I need you

The next poem focuses on the hard times I began to experience financial problems, repossessions, struggling with food, and unemployment. I have encountered many drawbacks while going through, I started to become depressed, stressed, and started to waver in my faith. I continued to read his word in spite of my difficulties and discovered that God will never lead me to something, if he is not going to bring me out of it. The "word of God tells me that "he will never leave nor forsake me (Duet 31:6) God is my provider and ensured me in his word that "But my God shall supply all your need according to his riches in glory by Christ Jesus (Philippians 4:19) I entitled this next poem "Lord I Need You."

Spiritual Poems of Encouragement for Your Soul

Lord I need you

Lord I need for you to see me through, I've been waiting anxiously to hear from you. I've been told if I worry don't pray, and if I pray don't worry. I'm in need of a right now breakthrough. You told me hold on and faint not in all I do. The struggle is on and I will continue to trust in you. Lord I need you to strengthen me so that I may grow. I will not dare question the molding process I'm your willing vessel, readily prepared to undergo. While I'm waiting I will meditate on your every word. My Praise is the key; I somehow didn't notice the transfer that spontaneously occurred for prayers were answered and not unheard. When I affixed my eyes back on you Lord I saw many miracles and unclosed doors. The word of God assures that there is no lack to the good and upright. I was too busy focusing on the storm ahead and unsure, my vision must have been altered, for the blessing in store was a greatly flooded river of constant Out Pour!
Don't Give up the blessing is on the way!

Chapter 5: Walking After Thee

The next poem is about my spiritual walk with God, the journey may seem long at times and become difficult, but it gets sweeter and sweeter every day. I have learned how to humbly submit to God. I learned that you submit by obeying his every word, and allow him to guide you through his spirit. God wants us to walk with him not ahead as he set the tone or pace for our lives. "I will instruct thee and teach thee in the way which thou shalt go: I will guide thee with mine eye (Psalms 32:8) I have entitled my next poem "Walking After Thee."

Walking After Thee

How I long to walk after thee I'll trust you to carry me through infinity, though the journey may seem long, I'm following you I'll never go wrong, eyes forward as I quickly pick up the pace. I'm from generation Jacob desperately seeking your face. I'll walk with the heart of integrity, clothing my mind with that which is noble you see. My eyes cannot possibly fathom, the things you have stored up for me, though the hills may seem high my dear, you mustn't give up. Grab hold to my words and begin to strut, God you ensured me in our little talk, "that you will never leave nor forsake me, my child just continue to walk, and you will see that child I've already predestined you to be, with the heart of a lion a bond stronger than that of mount Zion. Lord I will forever trust in you, because now I've realized. I'm not walking directly with my eyes it's my heart that's constantly chasing after you.

Hello Lord it's me

Chapter 6: What Happened?

The next poem is about the things I began to see every day, the ignorance of selfishness. God wants is to love him with all our hearts, minds, and souls. He wants us to also love our neighbors as ourselves. The two golden rules we are to embrace by pouring into God and our fellow brothers and sisters. The word of God lets us know "Jesus replied: "Love the Lord your God with all your heart and with all your soul and with all your mind, this is the first and greatest commandment. "And the second is like it: 'Love your neighbor as yourself (Matt 22:37-39) I entitled it "What Happened?

What Happened?

What happened to I need you, what
happened to people caring if you made it
through. Kind words like: "let me help you?
Thank you and I love you. I look around and
couldn't help but frown at the things I began
to discover, wondering how blind the world
have become not paying any cares or
attention to the sensitivities of our brothers.
The message was plain and spelled out clear,
even the blind and lame will adhere. "Love
thy neighbor "up lift one another in any
struggle, for we know them all so well. Stop
hating and killing and you will do swell.
Please carry out the commands that were
given, choose to love instead of hating
shown in your everyday living. Only time
will tell what everyone is made of, take a
closer look in the mirror before you ever
began to judge. Let us stop procrastinating
and we can make a difference in any
circumstance with just love. We can do it by
taking the time to listen, so the next time you
get a chance to change a situation. Don't

shake your head and walk off just yet, pay
close attention to that stranger you've just
entertained was the face of God, his
messenger clearly one of his angels.
Wake up!

Chapter 7: Forgivness

The next poem is about Forgiveness, Learning to forgive and let go allows God to do his perfect work in me. In this spiritual walk with Christ, I realized how much of self-need to die out, and once submission comes into play, the Holy Spirit takes control and rest completely. I have learned that there are times you need to overlook the small stuff. The small things are those that keep individuals hindered from obtaining the salvation of the lord. I recently learned that there is so much freedom in forgiveness. Forgive others and please do not hold grudges, let go and let God heal you. "But if you do not forgive others their sins, your Father will not forgive your sins (Matt 6:15)

Forgiveness

Did someone whisper something softly in the air? or was that just me being paranoid stuck in the middle of nowhere. I'm wondering how on earth I even managed to get here. I'm clearly in the state of unforgiveness; I really need someone to lift this heaviness because it is weighing me down. I'm miserable walking around trying to reverse this frown, Oh my how did I ever get stuck in this state. I'm pointing fingers at everyone but myself. I'm guilty deep down I feel like a filthy rag, I'm dirty. He, she, and they all ganged up on me. I'm really sick of all of my own excuses. I got one more nobody's running up to me to make amends or say sorry. What is the point of me even apologizing? When you don't say sorry you can stay trapped in an unforgiving state of mind that will surely keep you hindered and blinded.

The enemy loves a soldier whose mind is captivated. God loves you and wants you to love your neighbors unconditionally, not adopting the characteristics of Cain when angered didn't choose to refrain but quickly reacting in a sudden slain his brother able in cold blood, it's his spirit that cries out from the mud it's better to forgive and love. Signed sealed and delivered from the almighty above. God teaches us to forgive our brethren it's the only way to heaven. He told us constantly in his word but up to seventy-times seven

Chapter 8: I'm a Soldier

The next poem is about being accepting into God's Army as his soldier. I had the privilege to serve in the United States Army for 4 years. I now have a new position to soldier in God's Army; in this army you must be properly equipped. God has already giving us the victory, and the battle is the lord's. I have entitled this poem "Soldier "Put on the full armor of God, so that you can take your stand against the devil's schemes (Ephesians 6:11)

I'm a soldier

I'm a soldier in God's army Equipped and prepared to fight Satan the enemy. I'm armored down from head to toe ready and at any given moment to strike a devastating blow. Salvation is my headgear properly fit, loose straps fastened behind my ears. My waist is girded with his truths casting away all my fear. I will fight with ready fists not forgetting my breastplate of righteousness. My feet are forever sweet; God has prepped them with his gospel of peace. I already know we are fighting unseen enemies faces all messed up I'm taking down all beasts, with my shield of faith. Last but not least I will annihilate the enemy totally with the sword of the spirit for God himself have readily equipped every believer to hold a position to soldier in his Army..........
The battle is not yours

Chapter 9: Hell

The next Poem is about my experiences I had a basketball scholarship to be a part of the Morris College Women Hornets Basketball team. I tried it for almost a year, and realized I had enough schooling. I decided to go to New York after dropping out of college to be closer to my dad and find employment. I began to work three jobs KFC/Taco Bell, Kohl's, and Party City. I figured this would have been a substantial amount of income. I started partying and got introduced to the drug game, I would smoke pot and eventually I started to sell it. I would get off my place of employment and head to a friend's house to bag and sell pot. I was truly living my life in what I knew as the fast lane.

I did this for a while until one day I decided to get some lottery tickets from my everyday train station ride. On this particular day I decided to go on a bicycle. The bike did not belong to me but a neighbor. In Long Beach, New York there is a routine bicycle patrol program conducted by Long Beach Police department. The program helps to monitor the stolen bicycles in the city. When I came from purchasing the tickets I was asked "Ma'am is this bicycle? My reply was "Yes Sir. The Officers read me of my Maranda rights and I was arrested for possession of stolen property. I later found out that the bicycle was stolen, and my so called friend hid it from me. I was behind bars with a brazier full of marijuana, I was headed for hell. When I got released from jail I decided to enlist in the military. I had court and the judge ruled in my favor dropping the charges to a misdemeanor. I was blessed and did not recognize it.

Hell

Hello! You made it! How was the trip? They say it's hard to breathe and bleak darkness in the air, the constant hateful stares, life in hell is no fair, beasts approaching from every side of everywhere, even in pairs as if anyone cared. This is hell something no one could ever imagine to compare, the emptiness of darkness that takes you further into nowhere. There is no one stopping the nasty sulfuric smell that goes on and on. The pain is beyond complaining I just can't explain. Can somebody please stop all this screaming? Come here pitch me, I'll wake up soon cause I must be dreaming It's real I couldn't even count the demons I've encountered down here it's like they live and breed off my fear.

Hell has so many parts, I'm beginning to feel a sudden pain in my heart, oops I've just realized a dead soul doesn't have self-control could somebody pull me out of this black hole I feel like I'm in the deepest part of she'ol. I need some form of escape plan I'll give it a try by calling up the man, Hello God are you there? Can you hear me? Listen I'm sorry. And his reply to me was "I here you but it's a little too late my child you've made your bed now enjoy laying in it. You've rejected all of my ways; your time ran out now you're trapped in sin for an eternity. Heaven is a place filled with unconditional love, my sincerest regards from above. My invitation to you that's still living, Repent, Be Baptized, and filled with my spirit and you to will experience everlasting blessings.

Chapter 10: A Married Man

The next poem is during the times I was sinning in the act of adultery. I was messing with one of my friend's husband. The cheap lines like: "What she do not know will not her. When you sin you do the injustice before God first, and then your neighbor who was made in the image of God. Many people believe that sins will not go unpunished, but all sin is unrighteousness in the sight of God and carries a price. I was wrong and I admitted my faults to God asking him forgive me of my wrongs.

A Married Man

A moment of pleasure a kiss of desire took me further into a place of sin, I was beginning to fight fire with fire. I was single and fresh out of a relationship, I quickly begin to do my own thing, and I ran into a guy that simply caught me by surprise... He was my new fling, but it still was simply not enough to stop this thing. It started with just a mysterious date, but quickly turned into something more serious. I became a bit delirious every time he was around, news travel fast in a small country town. The word around town was this new lover I've thought I found was married. I began thinking to myself; oh lord what could I do to stop all of the madness and the countless secret Rendezvous? With Mr. you know who, I fooled myself into thinking it was a small sin. No big deal, sooner things really began to get out of hand. I needed to see him like every weekend, he was busy at home with his family being a husband and soon to be daddy, I mostly found myself stuck in bed waiting by the phone. maybe he'll call me if I adjusted the ringer on this telephone. I was only fooling myself I had a severe case of the jones. I began to fall in love, now this was not a feeling that I could just push away. I lay across the bed reminiscing on the sweet melodies of Shirley Murdock's as we lay. I was thinking about the deep mess I've allowed myself to sink in. Adultery is not right and in his sight its still sin. I've realized it's not only God that I've disappointed but I've also betrayed a very loyal friend. I needed to find a way out and God was my only escape. I sincerely prayed to God that he forgives me and make all of the chaos go away; I promise to serve him and began to slowly see my way. A word from the wise the next time you shopping around for a man. Take your time and never look upon a married man. Let God will be done in your life and he will send someone for you just keep the faith and listen to the words I've just given you.

Chapter 11: A Place for Me

I wrote this poem in memory of a very close friend and classmate "Vincent Omar Thomas. When I heard the news it was devastating, I began to suddenly remember everything crammed into a short film. Words cannot even express our friendship and how much you meant to me. Vincent your precious memories will forever live on in my heart. You handled everyone lives in whom you came in contact with care. You always had a way with people, and the imprint you left my friend will forever be remembered. The memory that I would truly miss about you was your big bright smile. I remembered you wore it all so well despite anything you may have faced. I love and miss you friend, until we meet again, sleep on in your better place.

A Place for Me

There is a place for me beyond the great blue
sky. A place God designed and purposed even
before the beginning of time. I know you're
burdened friends but you mustn't cry.

There many questions left unanswered sad
whispers of why the master knows best one of
his soldier's past life's final test. We all must
conquer the sudden sting of death. My race is
done but, you must continue to run. My journey
here is over, the new has just begun.

The place you and I dreamed of above the sun.
There may be a pause or void in your day,
remember my big bright smile if you may at the
start and close of each day. God took me in his
arms. I may be gone, but forever in your hearts.
He gave me a better place, a place beyond the
Stars.

Class of 1999

We love you Vincent

Michelle Stadard

Chapter 12: I am the Ladder

The next poem I entitled it I am the ladder. We all have a ladder to climb and on this Christian journey many things such as trials and tribulations and the cares of this life will try to stop us from reaching the top of it. We must keep our focus which is on Christ and he will help us obtain our destiny. The ladder of salvation takes us higher and higher in God. Many times we are all focused on what's going on with the next person; it is up to each individual to climb his or her own ladder.

I am the Ladder

I'm going to climb it with all of my might. I'm
talking about being consistent, like Jacob if it
means fighting all night or like the blind man
who kept striving and was made whole on that
road of Jericho. He encountered Christ was
healed and it changed his entire life. We were
born climbers that minute we submitted and gave
our lives to Christ. We are climbing to reach or
obtain a higher level, Yes in God we only move
up according to our measure of faith. It's
important that we stay focused, to ensure we do
not fall off or by circumstances lose our place.
We must look forward and not behind, keeping
the things of Christ constantly on our minds, his
statues will strengthen and help us endure. One
thing I must tell you, this is and individual climb,
so be sure your actions are adding up and you're
climbing this ladder of salvation for yourself.
We must continue climbing

Chapter 13: Change Within

The next poem is called "The Change Within, I have entitled it that for there is a change that takes place when you meet Jesus. The word of God tells is "Therefore if any man be in Christ, he is a new creature: old things are passed away; behold, all things are become new (2 Corinthians 5:17) I like to reflect on the Apostle Paul, and his life changing experience on the road to Damascus. Paul life was changed, for he met Jesus! And he could not go back down the same road in which he once traveled. God even changed his name from Saul to Paul, God knew the plans he had for his life, and his destiny was in Paul. The old name was Saul the persecutor of Christians and his new identity was the Paul the soul winner. When we have an encounter with God, our lives are forever changed and we began to do things differently, not with our own efforts but the help of the Holy Spirit.

The Change within

The change within is something that is simply
requested from the Almighty King Before it can
begin one must acknowledge all sin, how long
the purge take well it all depends, how fast a
person wants to be freed from iniquity, nothing is
forced for God accepts our pleas willingly. The
individual must know that God is righteous
unfailing, loving, equally and unconditionally.
He have a zero tolerance level when it comes to
sin, in spite of a rebellious people his love remain
unchanged sending his son Jesus as a ransom to
make amends, many struggle and make excuses
as if the load is carried alone, The answer is yes
and nothing else will just do, he took them on for
everybody the battle was won long ago down at
Calvary, he expressed his love but there is still
something required individually, the change that
takes place so one can live without worries for
eternity, Please listen carefully to the
instructions below, they are simple "Accept Jesus
Now! Without delay and others will see the light
shining brightly from within.

Let your love show!

Chapter 14:

I wrote this last poem concerning the eternal resting place of the people of God.

Heaven is simply indescribable in human language or terms. If the people of God live right heaven belongs to them. The Word of God tells us "However, as it is written: "What no eye has seen, what no ear has heard, and what no human mind has conceived" -- the things God has prepared for those who love him(1 Corinthians 2:9)

Conclusion

I thank everyone for taking the time to share the blessings of these special inspirational poems. I hope they be a blessing for you as they have been for me.

By. Michelle A. Stadard

Spiritual Poems of Encouragement for Your Soul

About Author

Michelle Stadard is a Native of Bishopville; SC She obtained her Bachelor's Degree in Christian Studies from Grand Canyon University in Phoenix, AZ. She is a Proud U.S Army Veteran; she is the Wife of Odimir Stadard, and full-time mother of four wonderful boys (Othello 15, Omani 12, Omar 6, and Odonis 6months). In her spare time she enjoys Writing Spiritual Poetry, Cooking, Reading, and spending time with friends and family.

Spiritual Poems of Encouragement for Your Soul

Michelle started writing poems at the age of 9 she has a passion for winning souls by ministering through her poems of Spiritual Encouragement Poems for our soul. These hand written elements are not only inspiring but give hope reaching down to the very depths of our souls. These poems were inspired by God to uplift his people and advance his kingdom.

Spiritual Poems of Encouragement for Your Soul

Pure Thoughts Publishing, LLC

www.PureThoughtsPublishingllc.com

52218758R00026

Made in the USA
Columbia, SC
01 March 2019